I0606046

To the Amdahl and Motomura families for embracing peace, and to our grandchildren Reid, Lucy, and Pip, may they grow into peacemakers too —C.S.

For my beloved Mo —A.Y.

Acknowledgments

I will never forget meeting Orval Amdahl and Tadahiro Motomura and their families and the St. Paul–Nagasaki Sister City Committee's help to arrange "The Return of the Sword" ceremony. My great thanks first go to Fumiko Yamaguchi, my Nagasaki "sword sister." Without Fumiko, the sword would have remained in Orval's closet. Nor would the sword have been returned without JoAnn Blatchley's partnership. As president of the St. Paul–Nagasaki Sister City Committee, JoAnn immediately saw the importance of the sword's return and helped turn a ceremony into a statement for world peace. To Bill Rannow, Japanese sword specialist, who helped us reveal the meaning of the sword. To the many people who lent their leadership to the Return of the Sword and to those who joined in as the audience, thank you for attending. Together, we created a healing community for all to witness. I am also indebted to my writing companions, Kristin Gallagher, Laurie Richardson Johnson, Deborah Eaton, and Marion Dane Bauer for their feedback to this story and for their friendship. A special tribute goes to Keiko Kawakami, senior teaching specialist of Japanese at the University of Minnesota, steadfast friend, translator, and cultural bridge builder, who helped me through all the projects we worked on together. Another huge thank-you goes to agent Rubin Pfeffer and editor Carol Hinz for embracing this story as a picture book. Finally, no acknowledgment would be complete without my heartfelt thanks to my husband, Kim Stelson, for his enduring belief in my work in Nagasaki and at home.

Domo arigato gozaimasu. どうもありがとうございます。

Text copyright © 2025 by Caren Stelson
Illustrations copyright © 2025 by Amanda Yoshida

All rights reserved. International copyright secured. No part of this book may be reproduced, stored in a retrieval system, or transmitted in any form or by any means—electronic, mechanical, photocopying, recording, or otherwise—without the prior written permission of Lerner Publishing Group, Inc., except for the inclusion of brief quotations in an acknowledged review.

Carolrhoda Books®
An imprint of Lerner Publishing Group, Inc.
241 First Avenue North
Minneapolis, MN 55401 USA

For reading levels and more information, look up this title at www.lernerbooks.com.

Backmatter photos by Kyle Whitney, courtesy of Caren Stelson.

Designed by Danielle Carnito.
Main body text set in Bailey Sans ITC Std.
Typeface provided by International Typeface Corporation.
The illustrations in this book were created with Adobe Fresco and Photoshop.

Library of Congress Cataloging-in-Publication Data

Names: Stelson, Caren, 1951– author. | Yoshida, Amanda, illustrator.
Title: Returning the sword : how a Japanese sword of war became a symbol of friendship and peace / [text by] Caren Stelson ; [illustrations by] Amanda Yoshida.
Other titles: How a Japanese sword of war became a symbol of peace and friendship
Description: Minneapolis : Carolrhoda Books, [2025] | Includes bibliographical references. | Audience: Ages 7–11 years | Audience: Grades 4–6 | Summary: "The powerful story of an American soldier and a Japanese family, centered on the return of a Japanese sword more than sixty years after the end of World War II" —Provided by publisher.
Identifiers: LCCN 2024048336 (print) | LCCN 2024048337 (ebook) | ISBN 9798765611531 (lib. bdg.) | ISBN 9798765673294 (epub)
Subjects: LCSH: World War, 1939-1945—Moral and ethical aspects—Japan. | Nagasaki-shi (Japan)—History—Bombardment, 1945. | Military occupation—Social aspects—Nagasaki-shi. | Amdahl, Orval. | Veterans—United States—Psychology. | Remorse. | Swords—Japan—History. | Motomura, Tadahiro. | Peace-building. | Forgiveness—Therapeutic use.
Classification: LCC D744.7.J3 S74 2025 (print) | LCC D744.7.J3 (ebook) | DDC 940.53/52—dc23/eng20250317

LC record available at https://lccn.loc.gov/2024048336
LC ebook record available at https://lccn.loc.gov/2024048337

Manufactured in Guang Dong, China by Dream Colour Printing
1-1011934-51775-3/7/2025

RETURNING THE SWORD

How a Japanese Sword of War *Became* a Symbol of Friendship and Peace

written by CAREN STELSON
illustrated by AMANDA YOSHIDA

CAROLRHODA BOOKS
Minneapolis

Nagasaki, Japan, 1945

Not long after the end of World War II, an American battleship steamed into a narrow harbor in Japan. Captain Orval Amdahl peered over the ship's bow at the city below.

Orval had been fighting in the war for a very long time. His body had never been wounded, but his heart ached from all that he had seen.

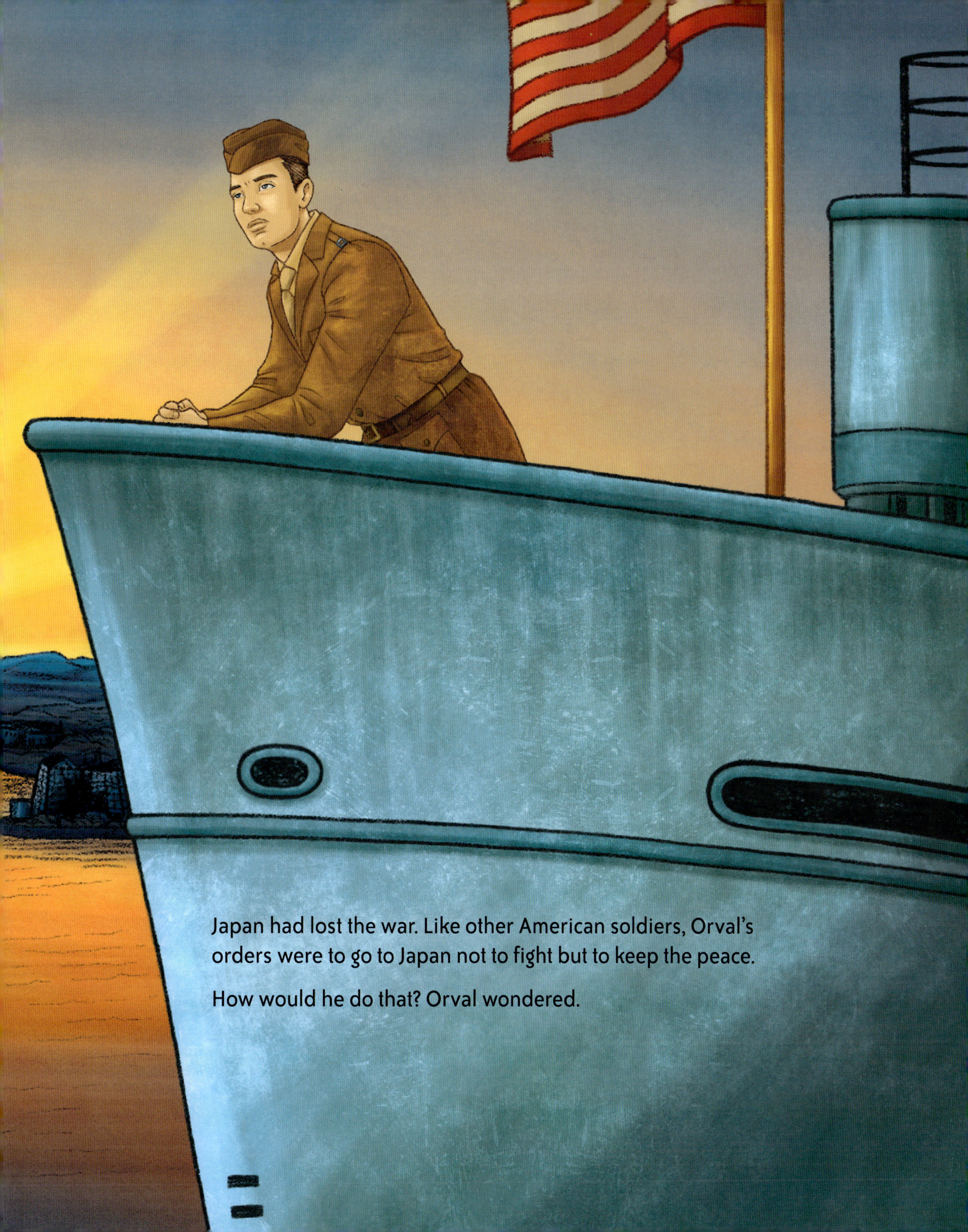

Japan had lost the war. Like other American soldiers, Orval's orders were to go to Japan not to fight but to keep the peace.

How would he do that? Orval wondered.

Orval marched off the ship's ramp into Nagasaki. The city had been destroyed by a terrible bomb. All around was dust and rubble. Wooden houses had turned to ash. Hospitals had collapsed. Schools had crumbled.

What Orval saw hurt his heart even more.

Every day Orval went on patrol. A man crossed the road pushing a wooden cart piled with his belongings. Orval stopped his jeep. So many people had lost nearly everything important to them in this terrible war.

What could Orval do to help?

He searched his heart, but he had no answers.

A group of children stood alongside the road. Orval stopped his jeep again.

“おはよう。おはよう。Ohayo. Ohayo,” the children shouted.

“Ohayo. Good morning,” Orval shouted back. *Ohayo* was the only Japanese word Orval knew.

The children’s clothes were ragged. Some were barefoot. They all bowed. A few bold ones stretched out their hands.

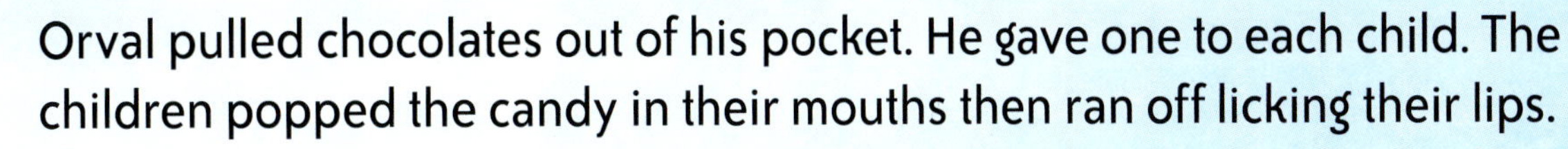

Orval pulled chocolates out of his pocket. He gave one to each child. The children popped the candy in their mouths then ran off licking their lips.

Were these children orphans? Had their parents been killed in the war?

What could he do for them?

Orval searched his heart, but again he had no answers.

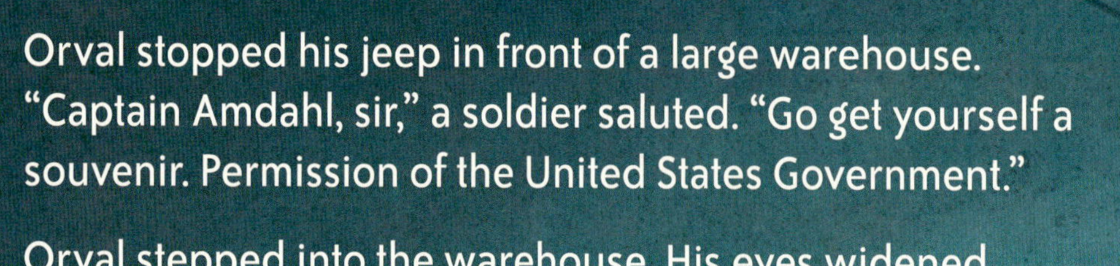

Orval stopped his jeep in front of a large warehouse. "Captain Amdahl, sir," a soldier saluted. "Go get yourself a souvenir. Permission of the United States Government."

Orval stepped into the warehouse. His eyes widened. Before him were swords piled eight feet high. Short ones. Long ones. Plain ones. Fancy ones for ceremonies. At the very top of the pile, a sword caught Orval's eye.

Standing on tiptoe, he stretched his long arms and carefully brought down the sword. He pulled the blade out of its leather scabbard and whistled, "What a beauty."

Other officers began to leave, swords under their arms. Orval slipped the blade back into the scabbard and followed them. A wooden tag tied to a brass ring dangled from the scabbard.

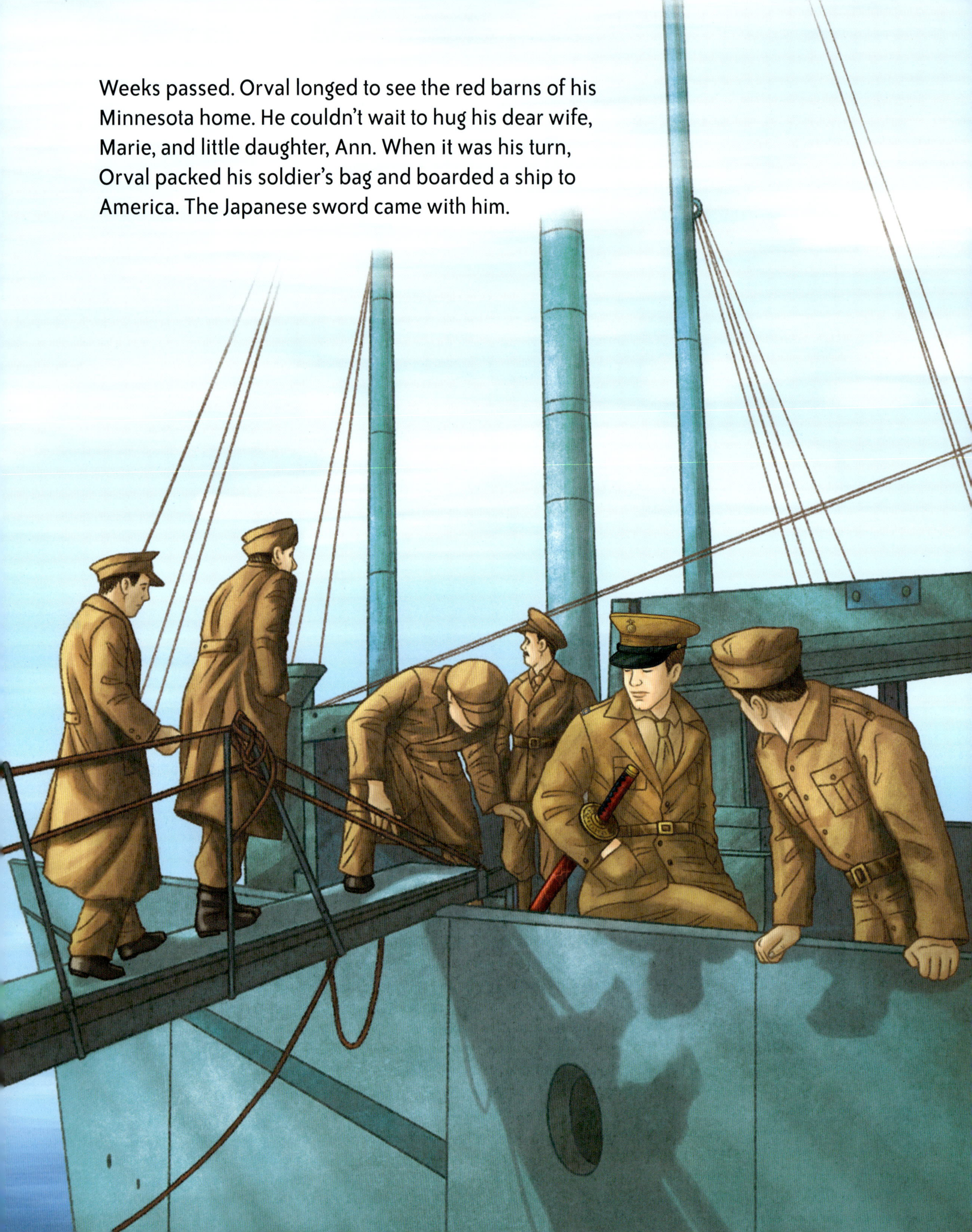

Weeks passed. Orval longed to see the red barns of his Minnesota home. He couldn't wait to hug his dear wife, Marie, and little daughter, Ann. When it was his turn, Orval packed his soldier's bag and boarded a ship to America. The Japanese sword came with him.

At home, everyone welcomed Orval. Friends clapped him on the back. Marie and little Ann fussed over him. Arm in arm, they walked into their house.

Upstairs, Orval took off his uniform, pulled off his soldier's boots, and stood the Japanese sword in his closet. He would try not to think about war again.

And he didn't, except in the middle of the night.

Enemy planes buzzed the skies.

Machine guns fired. Bombs exploded.

A city lay flattened.

Orval jerked awake from his nightmare.

In the morning, he peeked in the closet. The Japanese sword still leaned against the wall.

Maybe he should get rid of it.

One day a man knocked on his door. “I hear you brought back a sword from Japan. Mind if I see it?”

Orval climbed the stairs and came down with the sword.

“This sure is a beauty.” The man winked at Orval. He admired the sword’s handle, braided in gray silk. He stroked the well-stitched leather scabbard. He pulled out the blade and pointed to the wavy line along its edge. “A true Japanese sword. A real fine work of art.”

The man flipped open his wallet.
“How much do you want for it?”

Orval glanced at the wad of bills, then back at the sword. He thought about the wooden tag.

The man waited. And waited some more.

Finally, Orval shook his head. "No, I can't sell it. The sword isn't mine."

The man shrugged and left.

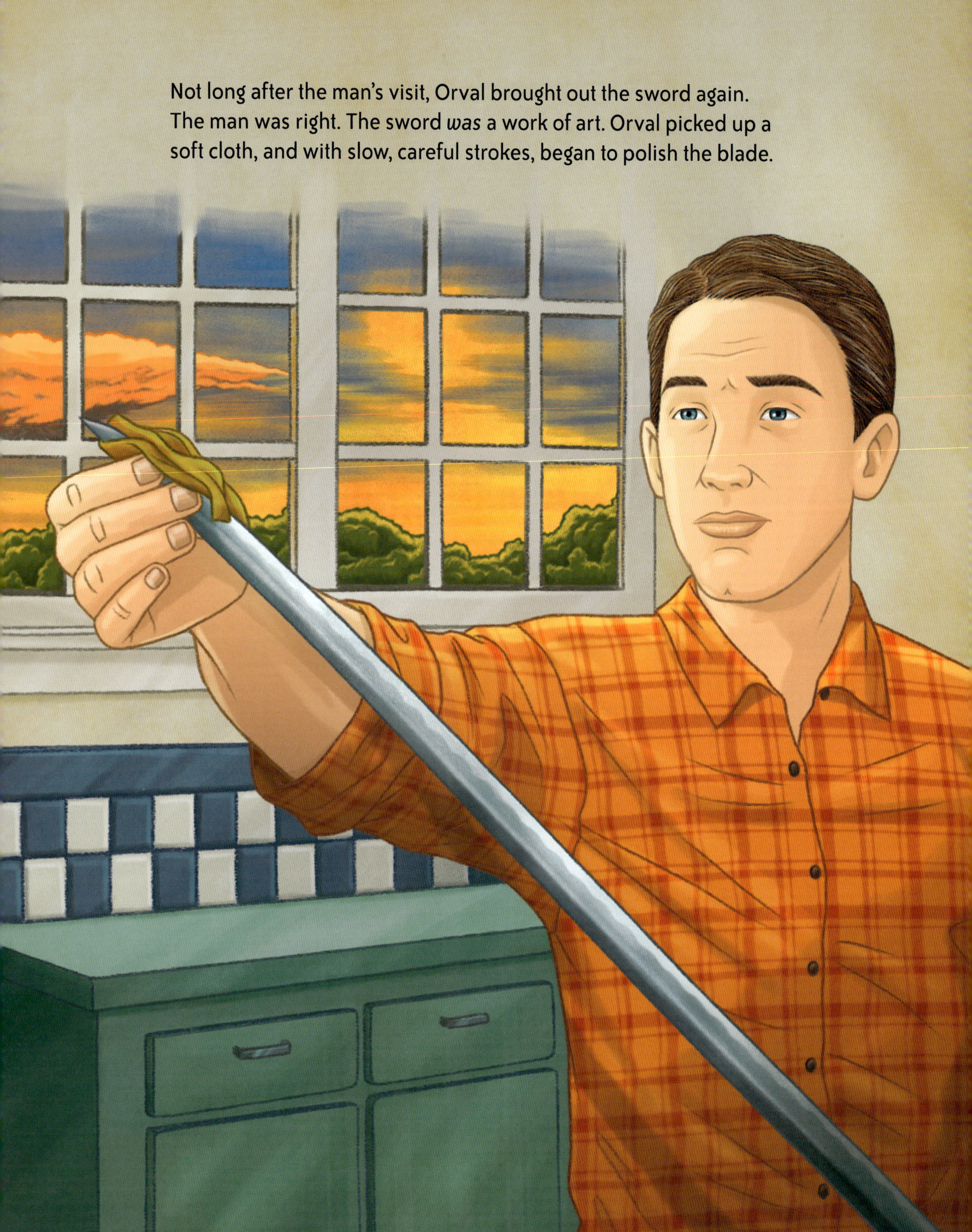

Not long after the man's visit, Orval brought out the sword again. The man was right. The sword *was* a work of art. Orval picked up a soft cloth, and with slow, careful strokes, began to polish the blade.

Orval's work at the lumber yard kept him busy. So did his growing family. Orval and Marie now had four children to care for. Still, each week, Orval cleaned the sword's blade. Every time he stared at the Japanese writing on the wooden tag, he wondered: Who wrote this? Another soldier? A father, like me?

Orval and Marie grew older. Their children grew up. Orval still polished the sword and stared at the tag. What could *he* do for peace? Orval held the sword up to the light. Suddenly, he had the answer.

But was it possible?

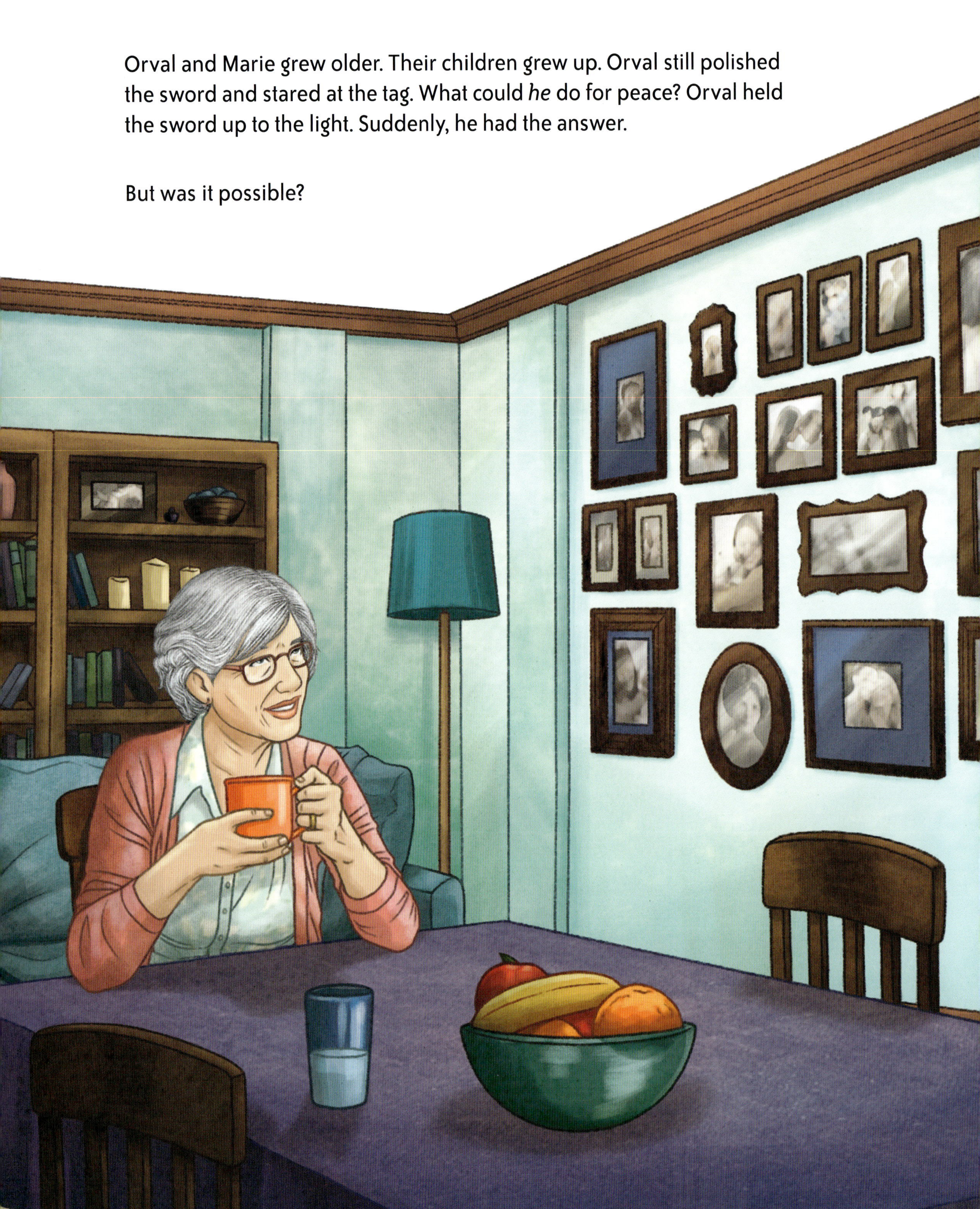

Then came the day
the doorbell rang.

Orval opened the door.

"Hello, Mr. Amdahl," said a visitor. "I'm the researcher who called you. Would you tell me more about your experience in Nagasaki after the war?"

The visitor and Orval sat at the kitchen table. Memories flooded back. Orval described the destruction. The people. The children. The eight-foot pile of swords . . . He stopped.

"Can I show you something?" Orval asked.

Orval climbed the stairs and came down with the sword in his hands.

"I've been polishing this sword for sixty-eight years," he told the visitor. "I want to return it to Nagasaki, if I can. To its rightful owner."

The visitor smiled. "I have a friend, Fumiko. She lives in Nagasaki."

The visitor took a photo of the sword. Of the tag. Of Orval. And she left.

The next day, the visitor called. “Fumiko found the sword’s family.”

Soon after, a letter arrived. It was from Mr. Tadahiro Motomura from Nagasaki. Fumiko added a translation.

Thank you for taking such good care of my father's sword. I would like to travel to America to meet you and to bring my father's sword home.

Orval closed his eyes.

Then he opened them wide. How would he greet Mr. Motomura?

Could he find the words in his heart he'd been waiting to say for so long?

Orval listened to his heart. He began practicing the only Japanese word he knew, and bowing, and what else he wanted to say—and *do*.

On the day of the celebration, Orval Amdahl and Tadahiro Motomura stood face to face.

Fumiko was there too, to translate.

"Ohayo, Motomura-san." Orval bowed.

"Ohayo, Amdahl-san." Tadahiro Motomura bowed too.

Together the two men walked into a small room where the sword lay on a table. The wooden tag was still tied to the scabbard.

Mr. Motomura traced the Japanese characters written on the tag with his finger. Slowly he turned and spoke.

Fumiko translated:

My father is no longer living, but this is his handwriting. My father talked very little about the war, but he told me about the sword and how important it was to him. At the end of the war, it hurt him to give it up.

Orval nodded.

I never dreamt I would see this sword. Our family thought American soldiers threw all the swords into the sea. We were surprised to learn our sword was in Minnesota, in your closet.

Orval nodded again.

My father would be so happy to know his sword is coming home.

Orval and Mr. Motomura walked into a large auditorium. A flute began to play. Three hundred people and several TV news crews waited for what would happen next.

Orval held the sword in his outstretched hands. In a voice strong and clear, he spoke the words his heart had longed to say:

"I return this sword to you in peace—peace with honor."

Mr. Motomura bowed.

Ninety-three-year-old Orval Amdahl bowed.

Their heads nearly touched.

Sixty-eight years after the war's end, Orval's heart had finally healed. But there was still one more thing Orval wanted to *do*.

He took a step forward and wrapped his long arms around Tadahiro Motomura.

And Tadahiro Motomura took a step forward and did the same.

THE STORY BEHIND THE STORY

The researcher who knocked on Orval Amdahl's door was me, the author of this book. Before meeting Orval, I had been writing a book about a woman who survived the Nagasaki atomic bomb as a child. Her name was Sachiko Yasui. During one of my trips to Nagasaki, Sachiko described the American occupation of Japan through her eyes as a then nine-year-old girl. I wondered: Were there any American veterans from my home state of Minnesota who had been in Nagasaki after the war's end? I made an appointment at the Minnesota History Center. Sitting in the oral history collection, I typed the word "Nagasaki." One name popped up—Orval Amdahl from Lanesboro. I called him the very next day.

"Oh sure, you betcha." Orval said in his best Minnesota greeting, "Come on down and visit."

At Orval's home, we talked for several hours about his war experience, particularly in Nagasaki. When Orval showed me the Japanese sword he kept in his closet, I knew he had a big story to tell.

After the interview, I drove home and immediately emailed photos of the sword and the tag to my friend Fumiko Yamaguchi in Nagasaki. "Would you like a mystery?" I asked. Fumiko wrote back, "Yes!"

It took Fumiko one day and one phone call to find the Motomura family, the original owners of the sword. The Japanese writing on the tag revealed the name and address of the family. With Fumiko's help as translator, Orval Amdahl and Tadahiro Motomura, the son of the original sword owner, exchanged letters. Orval's wish was slowly coming true.

On the United Nations International Day of Peace, September 21, 2013, three hundred people filled the Como Park auditorium in St. Paul, Minnesota, at an event organized by the Saint Paul-Nagasaki Sister City Committee. Among the special guests was Clifton Truman Daniel, the eldest grandson of President Harry Truman, who had made the decision to drop the atomic bombs on the cities of Hiroshima and Nagasaki. In his closing speech, Mr. Daniel summarized what the audience had come to witness: "It seems a small thing, giving back a sword that was taken as the spoils of war, but it symbolizes some of mankind's noblest traits—empathy, understanding, and honor."

Caren Stelson and Fumiko Yamaguchi at the Motomura family home in Nagasaki, Japan, in 2014. The sword is on display as part of the family altar.

Note: The direct quotations in the text and back matter come from my own notes and memories as well as from the resources listed in the bibliography.

MORE ABOUT ORVAL AMDAHL

Orval Amdahl grew up in southeastern Minnesota, in the small, rural town of Lanesboro. As a boy, he rode horses and plowed fields, went to Lanesboro's public schools, and eventually attended St. Olaf College in Northfield, Minnesota.

After the Japanese Navy attacked Pearl Harbor, Hawaii, on December 7, 1941, Orval joined the 2nd Marine Division, Artillery Group, eventually becoming a Marine captain. Orval fought a total of thirty-one months through terrible battles: Guadalcanal, Russel Islands, Marshall Islands, and Saipan.

On September 23, 1945, Orval's ship entered the narrow harbor of Nagasaki, twenty-one days after Japan had officially surrendered, and just over a month after the atomic bombing of Hiroshima and Nagasaki by the United States. In Japan's two-thousand-year-old history, the country had never been occupied by a foreign country, but in September 1945, American soldiers marched off their ships as an occupying force.

Orders came from the Supreme Commander of Allied Forces, General Douglas MacArthur, to confiscate all

Orval Amdahl returns the sword to Tadahiro Motomura in St. Paul, Minnesota.

weapons from Japanese homes. Sometimes the weapon was a sword, and often that sword was a family's treasure. The making of Japanese swords has a long history of artistry, material strength, precision, and symbolism. In hopes of someday retrieving their sword, a family would attach a surrender tag with the owner's name and home address, as Tadahiro Motomura's father had done. Once the weapons were warehoused, America officers were granted permission to take war souvenirs back home. The original owners never saw their swords again. The Japanese sword Orval returned is an exception.

Orval's story of the "Return of the Sword" flew around the world in newspapers and on television, radio, and social media. Letters arrived thanking Orval for his gift of peace and reconciliation. Some American World War II veterans wrote they also hoped to return their Japanese swords to their rightful owners, but without an identifying surrender tag, for them, it would be nearly impossible.

Less than two years after the sword's return, on February 17, 2015, Orval Amdahl died at the age of ninety-five. Orval's extended family, many friends, and American Legion veterans arrived for the funeral service. Orval's eldest son Ron stood next to a bouquet of white chrysanthemums from Nagasaki, holding a letter in his hand from Mr. Motomura. Ron read the letter out loud, pausing before reading Mr. Motomura's final sentence. "I sincerely promise to hand down this story of my father's sword from generation to generation in my family." Ron faced his family. "And I promise to do the same—to hand down from generation to generation the story of the sword my father returned."

If you have questions about returning World War II Japanese swords, flags, and other items to original owners, please contact the Obon Society (obonsociety.org), whose mission is to create peace and reconciliation across generations and nations.

A MESSAGE FROM TADAHIRO MOTOMURA

It has been eleven years since the Return of the Sword ceremony. Time really flies.

When I was a child, my mother told me about the sword several times. She told me that the sword, which my father had brought home when he returned from his service in the Japanese army, was very magnificent. However, it was confiscated when Japan surrendered at the end of World War II. After listening to my mother's story, I sometimes wished that I could have seen the sword for myself. But because so much time had already passed, I thought that it had probably been destroyed or melted into iron. I never imagined that it could have traveled all the way to the United States.

As time went by, I completely forgot about the sword. When I received a message about its whereabouts, I was really surprised to find out that it had been polished and cared for by someone for all of sixty-eight years and was still intact. I was also surprised to find out that the sword had been made in December 1941 (known in Japan at the time as Showa 16), when the Pacific War started. I feel a kind of destiny that it was returned in the peaceful era after all those years. Once again, I would like to express my gratitude to Mr. Amdahl, who carefully preserved and cared for the sword, considering it as a Japanese work of art. I would also like to express my gratitude to Ms. Caren Stelson, Ms. Fumiko Yamaguchi, and both St. Paul and Nagasaki Sister City Committees for their hard work to return the sword. Thank you very much for holding the Return of the Sword ceremony.

~Tadahiro Motomura, August 2024

BIBLIOGRAPHY

Adamek, Anton. "The Story of the Sword: Lanesboro Veteran Reconnects with Nagasaki," *Bluff County Reader*. September 16, 2013.

"After 68 Years, WWII Vet Returns Samurai Sword to Owner." WCCO News. September 21, 2014. https://www.cbsnews.com/minnesota/news/after-68-years-wwii-vet-returns-samurai-sword-to-owner/

Amdahl, Orval H. "Minnesota's Greatest Generation Oral History Project: Part II: Interview with Orval H. Amdahl." Minnesota Historical Society Collections Online. https://www.mnhs.org/search/collections/record/15d56a4c-440c-413b-933e-ff4cfba9e5fb

Anderson, Jim. "Across Years, Miles, Sword Returning Home," *Star Tribune*. September 21, 2013, https://www.startribune.com/across-years-across-miles-sword-returning-home/224629411.

Brock, Rita Nakashima, and Gabriella Lettini. *Soul Repair: Recovering from Moral Injury after War*. Boston: Beacon Press, 2012.

James Amdahl (second oldest son of Orval and Marie Amdahl) interviewed by phone by the author, February 10, 2021.

Karyl Amdahl Tammel (youngest daughter of Orval and Marie Amdahl) interviewed by phone by the author, February 9, 2021.

Marlantes, Karl. *What It Is Like to Go to War*. New York: Atlantic Monthly Press, 2011.

"Orval Howard Amdahl Obituary." *Legacy Remembers*. February 19, 2015. https://www.legacy.com/obituaries/postbulletin/obituary.aspx?n=orval-howard-amdahl&pid=174196399

"Return of the Sword." Minnesota History Society Facebook page. August 9, 2020. https://www.facebook.com/watch/?v=636722843622477

Shaw, Henry I., Jr. *Marine Corps Historical Reference Pamphlet: The United States Marines in the Occupation of Japan*. Washington, DC. Reprinted 1969. https://www.marines.mil/Portals/1/Publications/The%20United%20States%20Marines%20in%20the%20Occupation%20of%20Japan%20%20PCN%2019000411500.pdf

Stelson, Caren. "The Return of the Sword." *St. Olaf Magazine* 61, no. 1 (Winter 2014): 44–45.

Ronald Amdahl (eldest son of Orval and Marie Amdahl) in discussion with the author, January 27, 2021.

"War Bonds: A Soldier's Story Proves History Matters—and Sometimes Heals." *History Matters: For Members of the Minnesota Historical Society* 9, no. 3 (Winter 2014): 4–5.